ASKING·ABOUT·SEX
AND·GROWING·UP

JOANNA COLE

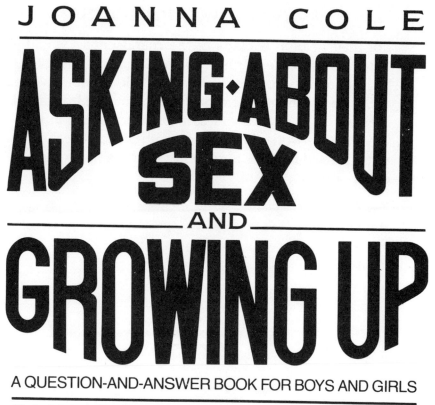

ASKING·ABOUT SEX AND GROWING UP

A QUESTION-AND-ANSWER BOOK FOR BOYS AND GIRLS

ILLUSTRATED BY ALAN TIEGREEN

Beech Tree Books / New York

· Acknowledgments ·

For their helpful readings of the manuscript, I would like to thank Louise Bates Ames, codirector of the Gesell Institute for Human Development; Bernice Berk, school psychologist at the Bank Street Laboratory School for Children; and Laura Kleinerman, a psychoanalyst in private practice in New York City who has worked extensively with preadolescents. Thanks also to David Reuther for sharing with me his expertise as an editor and as a parent.

Inquiries should be addressed to
William Morrow and Company, Inc.
105 Madison Avenue
New York, NY 10016.
Printed in the United States of America.
First Beech Tree edition, 1991
1 3 5 7 9 10 8 6 4 2
Library of Congress Cataloging-in-Publication Data
Cole, Joanna.
Asking about sex and growing up: a question-and-answer book for
boys and girls/by Joanna Cole; illustrated by Alan Tiegreen.
p. cm.
Includes index.
Summary: Uses a question-and-answer format to present sex
information for preteens.
ISBN 0-688-06928-2 (pbk.)
1. Sex instruction for children—Miscellanea. [1. Sex
instruction for children. 2. Questions and answers.] 1. Tiegreen.
Alan, ill. II. Title.
HQ53.C645 1988
306.7'07—dc19
87-26140
CIP AC

·CONTENTS·

·ASKING·ABOUT·SEX· ·AND·GROWING·UP·

·Introduction·

When a family can talk together about sex, there are a lot of benefits. The kids learn about an important part of life from people who love them and care what happens to them. The parents make sure their children find out what they need to know as they grow up. Everyone feels good because the "telephone lines" are open. No one has to be all alone with a question, a worry, or a problem.

But it's not always easy for parents and kids to talk. Some parents were raised in homes where sex was rarely, if ever, mentioned. They want to change that for their own kids, but it's hard to do. Parents are embarrassed or uncertain, and that can make kids feel embarrassed, too.

It can help if kids understand this about parents. Feeling some shyness about something as personal as sex is common—for adults *and* kids. Admitting that you feel awkward can make it easier to talk.

Some parents say, "My kids don't have any questions about sex." That is probably not true. The children most likely are interested but don't know how to bring up the subject. Perhaps it has never occurred to them that sex can be talked about openly. Parents can encourage discussions by letting kids know they are available. A parent might say, "Most kids your age have a lot of questions about sex. If you have any, I'll be glad to answer them."

It's good to remember that talking about sex is a personal matter. It's healthy to discuss it openly, but everyone has a right to his or her privacy. Parents want to be asked about growing up, but usually they don't discuss their own sex experiences with their kids. Kids want to be accepted when they bring up questions and feelings, but they don't welcome prying. On both sides, information and values can be shared while privacy is respected.

Some parents think that talking about sex means having one serious session in which the adult tells the child "everything." In fact, such a talk will not be all that helpful. Kids need to talk about sex and growing up many times as they reach different stages in their growth.

Often when sex comes up in conversation, parents automatically change the subject if kids are around. But a parent can use these opportunities to give information and to open discussions with kids.

Often parents feel they are not equipped to teach children about sex. How many adults remember exactly where the Fallopian tubes are, which hormone triggers ovulation, or exactly why a boy's voice cracks when it is changing? But this sort of information may not be what is really important when kids ask about sex. Biological facts can be looked up if they are needed, but they are often not what kids really want. They want a parent to assure them that wet dreams are normal, that puberty comes at different times for different kids, that masturbation does not do any harm. They need loving guidance, rather than an encyclopedia of sexuality.

The book you are reading now is intended for preteen kids. These kids already hear about sex all the time. What they hear and see on TV does not always give a healthy or even an accurate view of sexuality as it exists in everyday life. When kids learn about sex from adults they know and trust, they learn values and love along with the facts. They are then less likely to have sex prematurely and more likely to make responsible decisions based on their own best interests as they grow up.

Even though preteens need to be informed, talking with them about sex is not the same as talking with teenagers or adults. Most preadolescent kids have not yet experienced intense sexual drives. At their stage of development other issues, such as competence in school and sports and developing social relationships, are far more important than sex. They need to be informed, but they do not want to be overwhelmed by the entirety of adult sexuality. Therefore, the answers in this book are short, geared to the interests and needs of the age.

Some kids may be ready to read this book all at once. Other children may want to skip around from subject to subject. Or they may read a bit now, put the book away for a year, and rediscover it later, when they have new questions.

Parents will probably want to read this book along with their children, and will also find helpful some of the excellent books recommended below. As children move into adolescence, they may want to read some of the recommended books that deal with the special concerns of teenagers.

In addition to the information kids may get in school, from the media, and from their peers, kids need loving guidance about sex at home. I hope this book can be a helpful part of the talks between parents and kids in your family.

·Helpful·Books·

FOR KIDS:

Changing Bodies, Changing Lives (revised ed.) by Ruth Bell et al. New York: Vintage, 1987.

The Teenage Body Book by Kathleen McCoy and Charles Wibblesman, M.D. New York: Simon and Schuster, 1979.

The What's Happening to My Body Book for Boys by Lynda Madaras with Dane Saavedra. New York: Newmarket Press, 1984.

The What's Happening to My Body Book for Girls by Lynda Madaras with Area Madaras. New York: Newmarket Press, 1983.

FOR PARENTS:

How to Talk With Your Child About Sexuality: A Parent's Guide. Planned Parenthood, Faye Wattleton, president, with Elisabeth Keiffer. New York: Doubleday, 1986.

On Sex and Human Loving by William H. Masters, Virginia E. Johnson, and Robert C. Kolodny. Boston: Little, Brown, 1982, 1985, 1986.

Talking Sex With Your Kids by Lois B. Morris. New York: Simon and Schuster, 1984.

What We Told Our Kids About Sex by Betsy A. Weisman and Michael H. Weisman, M.D. New York: Harcourt, 1987.

· GROWING · UP ·

How do kids change?

As you grow up, your body changes. The first change everyone notices is that you keep getting bigger and taller and stronger. But your body grows in other ways, too. It changes from a child's body to an adult's body. It gets ready for reproduction—for the time when you may choose to become a parent.

What is puberty?

Puberty is that time in your life when your body changes. You change from a girl or boy to an adult woman or man.

What causes puberty to start?

The changes of puberty start when a gland in your brain releases a chemical called a hormone. This hormone travels in your bloodstream to your sex organs and stimulates them to release hormones of their own. All these hormones tell your body to start changing.

·FINDING·OUT·
ABOUT·SEX·

Is it normal to be curious about growing up?

It is natural for boys and girls to be curious about what will happen as they grow. You may have already noticed some changes in your body, and you probably want to know what the changes mean. If you have not yet started to develop, you still probably have questions to ask. You may not want to talk and think about growing up *all* the time, but if you are like most kids, you wonder what it will be like.

In addition to having questions about their own bodies, boys are usually curious about girls and girls are curious about boys. This is natural, too.

Is it okay to ask about sex?

Kids hear a lot about sex on TV shows, in the news, from other kids. Often everyone else seems to know all about everything. You might feel embarrassed to say that you don't know, but inside, you might still like a better explanation.

If you do ask about sex from a good, reliable source—a parent, a relative, a teacher—you might find out that some of the things you heard weren't quite right. You might see that some of the people who seemed to know everything didn't know so much after all. You might find out that you were worrying about something that you didn't have to worry about.

It is good for you to have straight, accurate information about sex. It helps you feel comfortable about yourself and your body, and it helps you make better choices about your life as you grow up.

·WHY·ARE·GIRLS'· ·AND·BOYS'·BODIES· ·DIFFERENT?·

One day Stacey's little sister saw her cousin Sam in the bath-tub. She pointed to his penis and asked, "Why don't I have one of those?"

Stacey couldn't help smiling. She told her little sister that boys and girls are different. Boys have sex organs on the outside where they are easy to see. Every girl is born with her own sex organs, but they are not as easy to see as a boy's. Some are inside her body, and some are on the outside, between her legs.

The sexual parts of our bodies are designed by nature for reproduction—having babies. A man and a woman are both needed to create a baby, but each sex has a different part in the process. That is why males' and females' bodies are made differently.

Of course, not every person chooses to be a mother or a father, but all people have sex organs, and everyone has sexual thoughts and feelings. Sex is a natural part of being a person.

What sex organs does a girl have?

Inside her body a girl has two ovaries—oval storage areas for egg cells that may someday grow into babies. She has a uterus—or womb—where a baby grows before it is born. And she has a vagina—a passage that leads from the outside of her body to her uterus. Just inside the vagina is the hymen— a thin web of skin that partly blocks the opening.

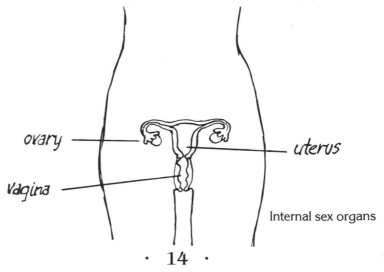

ovary — uterus

vagina

Internal sex organs

Outside her body, between her legs, a girl has a moist area called the vulva. At the front of this area is the opening that lets out urine. Just behind this, there is another opening—the entrance to the vagina, which leads to the uterus. Along the sides of the vulva are folds of skin called labia. There are two sets of folds, the inner labia and the outer labia. Toward the front, the labia join together in a V shape. In the V made by the inner labia, there is a small bump called the clitoris. This is very sensitive and feels good when a girl touches it, or the skin around it.

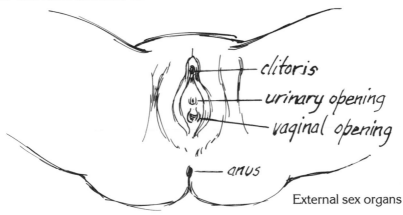

clitoris
urinary opening
vaginal opening
anus

External sex organs

Can a girl see her sex organs?
A girl can't see the organs inside her body, but she can use a small mirror to see her outside sex organs.

Does a girl have any other sex organs?
When a girl starts to become a woman, the area around her nipples will grow into breasts, which can make milk for a baby. Many women enjoy having their breasts caressed, and most men think a woman's breasts are beautiful.

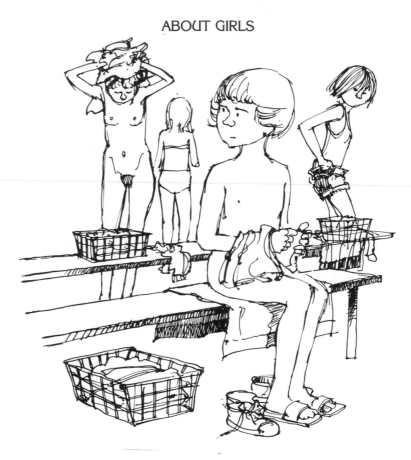

HOW GIRLS GROW UP

In the dressing room at the pool, Ellen saw that some girls her age were developing breasts. Others had soft hair growing between their legs or under their arms. Ellen was still flat, and she had no body hair. She worried that she would never grow up.

Ellen felt a lot better when her mother told her that the women in her family usually started developing a little late. Starting early doesn't mean your breasts will be larger or you will be taller.

Between the ages of about nine or ten to about sixteen, a

girl's body gradually changes. Her breasts grow, body hair comes in, she gets a lot taller, her body shape changes, and she gets her first menstrual period. For different girls, these changes happen at different times, but most girls have a mature body by their midteens.

What is usually the first change that happens to girls?

For most girls, the first change of puberty is the growth of the breasts. This growth usually begins around age eleven, but it can happen as early as eight or nine or as late as fourteen.

How do breasts grow?

When the breasts first begin to grow, the area right around the nipple gets larger and pushes out in a small mound. As times goes on, the whole breast becomes larger and fuller.

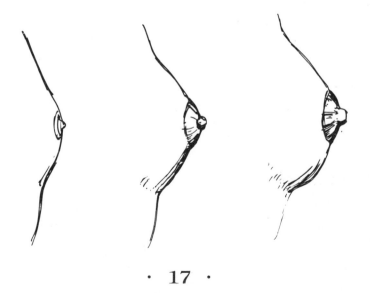

Is breast growth always the first change?

No. Although breast growth comes first for most girls, the first change for others may be the growth of body hair in the crotch or underarm area. It is normal if you begin either way.

Are larger breasts better than smaller breasts?

Some people, especially in the past, believed that women with larger breasts were more attractive. When your parents and grandparents were growing up, many girls and women believed that boys and men would not like them if their breasts were small. Today we know that this idea is silly. Being attractive does not depend on the size of one part of the body.

What if one breast seems larger than the other?

Sometimes a girl worries because one breast seems larger. However, this is normal. The larger breast is simply growing a little faster, and the other one will catch up in a short time.

Do breasts hurt?

Breasts and nipples do not hurt, but they are sensitive, so women try to avoid having their breasts bumped or hit. Some girls find that their nipples are especially tender while they are growing. Most do not feel anything different.

What are breasts for?

After a woman gives birth, special glands in her breasts begin to make milk for the baby. Women can choose to breast-feed their babies or to feed them with a bottle.

Do women with larger breasts have more milk?

Every woman has the same number of milk glands, no matter what size her breasts are. A mother's body makes the right amount of milk for the baby whether her breasts are large or small.

Why do women wear bras?

It is not necessary to wear a bra, but many women prefer to. Some women—especially those with larger breasts—feel more comfortable with the support of a bra and think their breasts look nicer in a bra. Others feel quite comfortable going without a bra.

When do girls start growing taller?

At an average age of eleven or twelve, most girls have a growth spurt when they grow extra fast. Girls start on their growth spurt about two years before boys do. So for a while, most girls are taller than boys their age. While girls start growing before boys do, they also stop sooner, so boys catch up. Most boys end up being as tall as or taller than most girls.

How does a girl's body change shape?

As a girl goes through puberty, her breasts get larger and her hips get wider, so her waist seems smaller. Overall, her body becomes more rounded, and her figure takes on the "curves" of a woman's body.

What body hair does a girl get?

A girl gets pubic hair in the crotch area and hair under the arms. In addition, the hair on her arms and legs may get longer and darker.

How do a girl's sex organs grow?

Both inside and outside her body, a girl's sex organs grow larger as she grows up. The uterus gets larger, and the ovaries grow and begin to get ready for releasing egg cells.

Outside, the inner and outer labia of the vulva become fleshier, and the vagina and clitoris get larger and more noticeable.

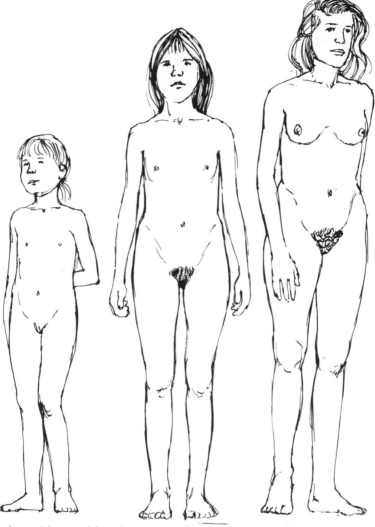

As a girl gets older, she grows taller, and her body changes shape.

What happens when a girl gets her menstrual periods?

When a girl or woman menstruates, blood flows from the uterus and out of the vagina. The period usually happens about once a month and lasts from three to seven days.

· 21 ·

Why do girls and women have periods?

Menstruation is part of a cycle that the female body goes through about every twenty-eight days to make the body ready for having a baby. The uterus is lined with a thick layer of tissue full of nourishing blood. If a woman becomes pregnant, the fertilized egg cell plants itself in this lining and begins to grow into a baby. Then the woman stops having periods and does not menstruate again until after her baby is born.

If a girl or woman is not pregnant, there is no use for the lining, and it flows out as menstrual blood. This happens over and over again during a woman's life.

The menstrual cycle

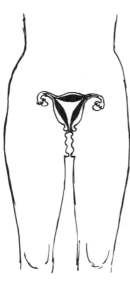 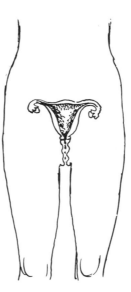 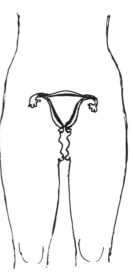

1) The lining of the uterus gets thicker.

2) If the egg cell is not fertilized, the lining flows out.

3) Then the lining builds up again.

Do periods always come every twenty-eight days?

Not always. Some girls and women have regular periods every twenty-eight days. Others have regular periods that come at other intervals—say every twenty-three or twenty-six or thirty or thirty-five days. But many girls' and women's periods are not regular; they start a few days earlier or later every month.

If a girl keeps a record of her periods on a calendar, she can tell what her pattern is.

At what age do most girls get their first period?

Most girls start menstruating around the age of twelve and a half, but this is just the average age. Some girls start as early as ten and a half. Others do not begin until fifteen and a half.

Is having your period like urinating?

Menstruation is different because the fluid comes from the vagina, not the urinary opening. It is also different because menstrual fluid drips out slowly over several days and is not under the person's control the way urinating is.

Does it hurt to menstruate?

Many girls don't feel anything different during their period, but some girls may get mild cramps in the abdomen. These usually do not last long, but if you are too uncomfortable, a doctor can help.

How does a girl get ready for her first period?

Usually a girl's mother helps her prepare for her first period. At the drugstore or supermarket, you can buy pads to absorb the menstrual flow. These have adhesive on one side and stick to the crotch of your underpants.

What are tampons?

Tampons are small plugs of absorbent material that are inserted inside the opening to the vagina. When the tampon is inserted properly, it cannot be felt, and it cannot fall out. A short string is usually attached to the tampon and hangs outside. The tampon can be removed by pulling on the string.

The advantage of a tampon over a pad is that the flow is absorbed inside the body, so it may be neater.

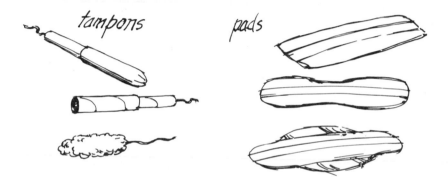

Can girls use tampons, or are they only for women?

Most girls can learn to use tampons. There are directions to follow in the box so a girl can learn how, and there are slender tampons that are easier for a young girl to use.

Because there is a disease called toxic shock syndrome (TSS), which has been connected to using tampons, it is best not to wear one all the time. You can reduce the risk of TSS by *alternating* tampons with pads. Some women use tampons during the day, or when they play sports, and wear a pad at night.

Is it okay to take a bath or shower during a period?

Yes, it is even okay to go swimming. Menstruation is not an illness. The best way to handle a period is to get out and do things, get exercise, and live your normal life.

Is it a lot of trouble to have a period?

Taking care of yourself during menstruation takes a little thought and effort, but, like keeping your hair combed, your fingernails neat, and your clothes clean, menstruation is something that all girls and women learn to manage as they grow up. It's not that difficult.

Does a woman have periods all her life?

No. At around age forty-five or fifty, women stop menstruating and can no longer have babies. This is called menopause.

How do girls feel about getting their period?

Every girl has her own feelings about menstruating. If a girl has not been told about it, she may think she has been injured when she gets her first period. This can be a very scary experience.

If a girl knows that menstruation is a normal part of being a woman, she will be proud because it means that she is growing up.

Does a girl become a woman when she starts to menstruate?

A girl still has a lot of growing up to do before she becomes an adult woman who can make grown-up decisions. Once a girl has begun menstruating, it is possible for her to become pregnant and have a baby, but she is not ready to take on the responsibility of motherhood yet. She still has a lot to learn about being a girl before she becomes a woman.

· 27 ·

·ABOUT·BOYS·

What sex organs do boys have?

A boy has a penis and two testicles—oval-shaped organs where sperm cells will someday be made.

The testicles are inside a pouch of skin—the scrotum—between the legs.

At the end of the penis there is a srnall opening where urine (and, someday, sperm cells) can come out.

The penis is very sensitive and feels good when you touch it.

Why do some penises look different?

When a baby boy is born, the end of the penis is partly covered by a piece of skin called the foreskin. Sometimes an operation is performed on babies to remove the foreskin. This operation is called circumcision.

If a boy is circumcised, his penis will look different from that of a boy who was not circumcised. But their penises are not really different. They work the same and feel the same.

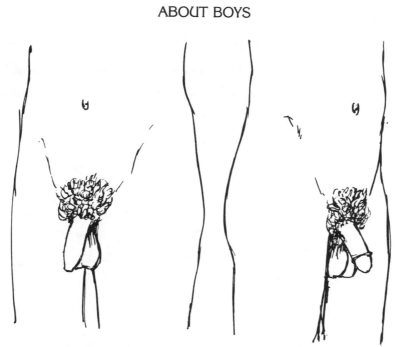

uncircumcised   circumcised

What is an erection?

Usually, a boy's penis is soft. The inside consists of spongy tissue; it does not have any bones. When the spongy inside of the penis becomes filled with blood, the penis gets larger and harder and stands up. This is called an erection.

When do boys have erections?

A boy can have an erection in many different situations. It can happen when he touches his penis, or when he thinks about sexy ideas. It can happen when his bladder is full, when he is asleep, or when he wakes up in the morning. It can happen when he has strong feelings of any kind—when he is nervous or scared or even just excited about playing a game.

All men and boys have erections. Even baby boys have them. They are a natural part of being a male.

· **29** ·

HOW BOYS GROW UP

In the shower one day, Mark noticed that his testicles were bigger than before and that the skin of his scrotum was getting wrinkled.

He wondered if this was normal, and since his penis was still small, he wondered why it had not started growing, too.

His older brother told him that the testicles usually begin to grow first, about a year before the penis starts to grow or any other bodily changes occur.

Between the ages of about eleven and sixteen or seventeen, a boy's body changes into a man's body. His testicles become larger and hang lower and his penis grows larger. He has a growth spurt and gets much taller, his voice deepens, his shoulders grow broader and his muscles get larger, he gets body hair and a beard, and his body begins to produce sperm that can combine with an egg cell to start a baby.

When does the penis begin to grow?

About a year after the testicles start their growth, the penis becomes longer and thicker. It also changes color, becoming slightly darker and, in light-skinned boys, redder.

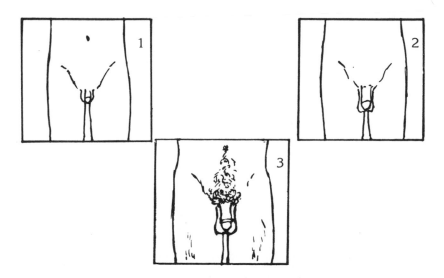

From about age eleven or twelve to sixteen or seventeen, a boy's penis and testicles gradually grow larger.

Why does one testicle hang lower than the other?

If both testicles were at the same level, they would bump together as a boy walks. Since testicles are very sensitive, this could be painful. One testicle usually hangs lower so this will not happen.

Is there a normal size for a penis?

In grown men, the average size for an erect penis is about six and a half inches. Some are a few inches longer, and some are slightly smaller.

If a man's penis is bigger than average when it is soft, will it also be bigger when it is erect?

Not necessarily. Penises that are smaller when soft usually add *more* inches when they become erect, and those that are larger usually add *fewer* inches when they get erect. You can't tell how big a penis will be when it becomes erect by looking at it when it is soft.

Is the size of a boy's or man's penis very important?

No. The size of the penis does not affect a boy's or man's life much at all. But some boys worry about it because of silly stories they hear from other kids. For example, they may hear that men with bigger penises have more sperm, that they are more manly, or that women enjoy making love with them more. None of these stories is true. Men with smaller penises can be just as good lovers as men with larger penises, and whether a man is "masculine" depends much more on his personality and self-confidence than it does on the size of his penis or any other part of his body.

When do most boys start growing taller?

Most boys start having a growth spurt when they are thirteen or fourteen, a couple of years after their testicles first start growing. A growth spurt means that they grow extra fast for a few years—usually about three and a half inches a year but sometimes as much as five inches a year.

Girls usually have their growth spurt about two years earlier, so for a year or two many girls are taller than most boys their age.

Do boys get stronger as soon as they get taller?

Not always. Sometimes, when boys are in the middle of growing, they get taller so fast that their muscles don't have a chance to keep up. Then a boy may seem weaker than he was before. This effect is only temporary. Before long, the muscles catch up with the rest of the boy's body.

How does a boy's shape change?

Size isn't the only change that happens during puberty. As boys grow, the shape of their body changes, too. Their shoulders get wider, and this makes their hips seem narrower. In addition, the muscles of their arms, legs, and shoulders get bigger, and they get much stronger.

When do boys get body hair?

About a year after the penis begins to grow, boys usually notice hair coming in at the base of the penis. This is called pubic

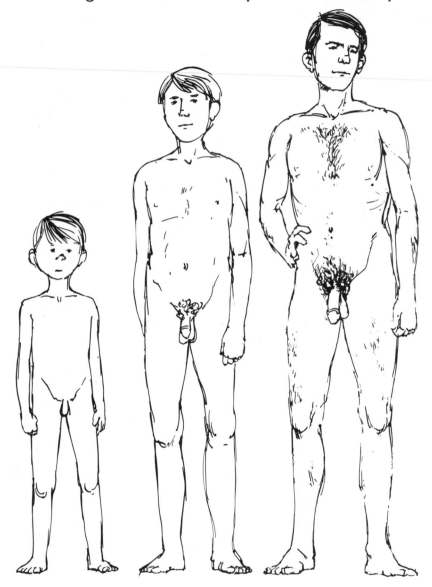

As a boy gets older, he grows taller, and his body changes shape.

hair. At around the same time, the hair on the arms and legs gets longer and darker.

Later, boys get underarm hair and may get hair on their chests and backs. For most boys, the last change is the growth of a beard. (As with the other changes of puberty, this may happen at different times in different boys.)

Do some boys have changes in their nipples during puberty?

Yes. About two-thirds of boys get hard little bumps under their nipples, which are sometimes called "breast knots." If boys haven't been told about these bumps, they can get awfully worried about them. In fact, many boys get scared that they are turning into girls. Of course, this cannot happen.

"Breast knots" are normal, and they are only temporary. They go away within eighteen months—usually sooner than that.

How does a boy's voice change?

When a boy is about fourteen or fifteen, his Adam's apple— voice box—grows larger. The vocal cords inside get thicker and longer, and this makes his voice deeper. While the voice box is growing, some boys find that their voices "crack" every once in a while. This means that the voice goes from normal to high and squeaky all of a sudden. Voice "cracking" can be very embarrassing to some boys, but it is temporary and goes away before too long.

What are sperm?

Sperm are special cells that are produced in the testicles. Every day, a male's body makes millions of sperm cells, each one of which can combine with an egg cell in a woman's body to start a baby.

Can you see sperm?

Sperm are so tiny that they can be seen only through a microscope. Each sperm cell has a head, a midpiece, and a tail. A sperm cell can swim through liquid by lashing its tail.

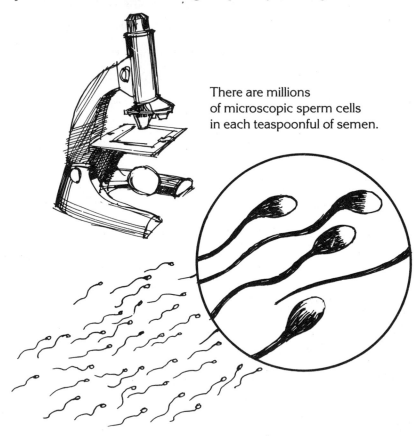

There are millions of microscopic sperm cells in each teaspoonful of semen.

At what age does a boy's body start to make sperm?

A boy's testicles start producing sperm when he is about thirteen, but because every boy develops at his own speed, this can happen a year or two earlier or a year or two later.

How do sperm leave a boy's body?

Once a boy's body begins making sperm, he will start having ejaculations from time to time. When a boy ejaculates, a thick, white liquid called semen comes out of the opening in the end of his penis. Mixed in the semen are millions of microscopic sperm cells. Even though there are so many sperm, they are so tiny that they fit in a small amount of semen—about one teaspoonful in each ejaculation.

When does a boy ejaculate?

Kids sometimes wonder if boys ejaculate when they are urinating. The answer is no. Urine and semen cannot come out of the penis at the same time. A special valve at the base of the bladder closes off the urine during ejaculation.

A boy usually ejaculates when he is masturbating—that is, rubbing his penis for pleasure. He will also ejaculate when he is having a wet dream.

What is a wet dream?

Sometimes, boys ejaculate in their sleep without being aware of it. This happens from time to time to all boys and men. Often a boy will remember having a sexy dream, and that is why nighttime ejaculations are called wet dreams. Often, however, there is no memory of a dream.

Most boys are embarrassed when they wake up and find semen on their pajamas or sheets. It may help to remember that parents know that nighttime ejaculations are normal and happen to all boys as they are growing up.

How do boys feel about wet dreams?

If a boy hasn't been told about nighttime ejaculations, he may be afraid he has a disease when it happens the first time. Or he may just be embarrassed. But if he has been told that wet dreams are normal, a boy will feel proud because he knows he is growing up.

Does a boy become a man when he begins to have ejaculations?

When a boy begins making sperm and having ejaculations, his body is like a man's in one way: His sperm can start a baby growing in a woman's body.

But most boys are about thirteen or fourteen when they begin ejaculating. A thirteen-year-old boy is not ready to take on the responsibilities of an adult. He can start a baby, but he cannot be a responsible father and husband. He needs time to be a boy before he is ready to be a man.

·TOUCHING·FEELS·GOOD·

Before he falls asleep at night, Greg sometimes rubs his penis. He likes the feeling it gives him—a wonderful feeling that is not like any other. It makes him feel very excited and then very peaceful and drowsy.

Greg's body and feelings tell him that getting pleasure from touching his penis is good. But he has heard some people say it is wrong to do it. He wonders if they are right.

Is it normal to touch your sex organs for pleasure?

Yes. Most people—girls and boys, men and women—touch or rub their sex organs at one time or another in their lives. Many people do it frequently. Touching your sex organs for pleasure is called masturbation.

Why do some grown-ups tell children it is wrong to masturbate?

People have different ideas about sex, depending on what they were taught as children. Some people were told years ago that masturbating is wrong, and they still believe it.

If adults tell you it is bad to touch yourself, remember that this may have more to do with *their* feelings than with what is right or wrong for *you.*

Does everyone masturbate?

Most people masturbate, but some don't have much interest in it. Others have a religious reason for not masturbating. Some people masturbate at certain times in their lives but lose interest at others. Although many young children masturbate, others do not do it at all until they are older.

It is normal to masturbate, and it is normal not to masturbate. Whichever way makes you happy is the right way for you.

How do girls and boys masturbate?

Boys usually make a fist around the penis and rub up and down. Girls usually use their fingers to rub the clitoris or the area around the clitoris.

Sometimes boys and girls move their sex organs against another object, such as the bed or a pillow.

Why do people usually masturbate in private?

In our society, sexual behavior is done in private out of consideration for others. Privacy also protects the person who is masturbating from being interrupted in his or her intense feelings.

Private does *not* mean "secret" or "sinful."

What is an orgasm?

Often a girl or boy may have a special feeling of pleasure while he or she is masturbating. This feeling is called an orgasm, or climax. An orgasm lasts for only a few seconds, but for both boys and girls it is a very powerful feeling.

For boys and men, the orgasm usually happens during ejaculation—the release of sperm—although some boys may have orgasms without ejaculating. Girls and women can have orgasms but they do not ejaculate.

For many girls and boys, orgasms may not happen until after puberty. For others, orgasms are just not very important. They enjoy masturbating without them.

Can it hurt you to masturbate?

It is not harmful to rub your sex organs for pleasure. It does not make you lose interest in the opposite sex, nor does it make boys run out of semen. These ideas and others like them are just plain silly.

If you enjoy masturbating, there is no reason you should not do it.

Can a person masturbate too much?

No. A person's body tells him or her when it is time to stop. Masturbating just doesn't feel good anymore at that time. When your body is ready again, you may feel like it again.

Masturbating a lot does not do any harm, but it may be a sign that you are trying to make yourself feel better when you are tense or unhappy about something. In that case, it is more important to try to get help with that problem than it is to worry about masturbating.

Is it normal to have daydreams and sexy ideas?

Yes. Most people have daydreams about sex now and then. Boys and girls think about going out on dates, hugging, kissing, or having sex.

Sometimes kids daydream about doing something they would not feel right about doing in real life. For instance, they may imagine making love with a teacher, a friend of their parents, even a relative.

Kids often worry about daydreams like these, but they are normal. The important thing to remember is that thinking about something and actually doing it are very different. Your daydreams are your private property. You can have them in private without feeling guilty.

·WHAT·IS·A·CRUSH?·

Every time Sharon sees Josh, she can't stop looking at him. She likes the way he walks, the way his hair grows, the way he smiles. She hopes that he likes her, too, and when she's alone, she daydreams about him.

When a boy or girl is attracted to someone like this, it is called a crush. Crushes are the first romantic feelings kids have as they are growing up.

How long does a crush usually last?

Sometimes kids have a crush on someone for a long time, but usually their feelings change after a few weeks or months and they become interested in someone new.

Does everyone have crushes?

Some kids have many crushes and spend a lot of time thinking about them. Other kids have very few. But almost everyone has a crush at one time or another.

Why don't adults take kids' crushes seriously?

Adults see a crush as a passing thing, and for this reason they may make light of it or even make jokes about it. Adults who do this, however, are not being very sensitive to kids. Even though preteen kids are not ready to have long-term relationships like marriage, their *feelings* can be just as strong as adults' feelings, and these feelings deserve respect.

Why do kids laugh about sex or tease other kids about having a crush on someone?

For both boys and girls, having new sexual feelings makes life more exciting. But it can make things more complicated, too. Kids are curious about sex, but, at the same time, they may feel a little guilty or embarrassed about it. So they laugh and make jokes about sex to hide their embarrassment. Jokes about sex *can* be very funny, but if they are just a cover-up for feelings people are ashamed of, they are usually not so funny.

If someone teases you about a crush, that person probably has tender feelings of his or her own—feelings he or she wants to hide. By making fun of someone else, the teaser hopes people won't notice that he or she might have a crush on someone, too.

No matter who may tease you, feeling attracted and loving toward a special person is an important part of becoming a mature person. It is nothing to be ashamed of.

Do kids ever have crushes on people of the same sex?

Yes. While it is typical for girls to "like" boys, and for boys to "like" girls, kids often have strong feelings of attraction for a person of their own sex—especially for someone who seems glamorous or exciting. A girl may be "in love" with a female teacher she admires especially. A boy may have feelings for a man or older boy he looks up to.

When kids hear about homosexuals—adults who have sexual relationships with people of their own sex—they may jump to the conclusion that because they have a crush on a same-sex person, they will be homosexual when they grow up. But this is not usually true. Many boys and girls have crushes on people of both sexes as they are growing up. (To read more about homosexuality, see page 73.)

When do girls and boys start dating?

Most kids are ready to start dating by their midteens. Of course, some kids of that age may not be interested in dating yet, and, if they are not, there is no reason to rush things.

Going out on a date with someone of the opposite sex is a lot of fun, but it takes experience to know what to say and do. Preteen kids get this kind of practice best in groups of boys and girls.

Is sex appeal the only reason for boys and girls to like each other?

Definitely not! Romantic attraction is often part of friendships between boys and girls and between men and women. But it is not the only part.

WHAT IS A CRUSH?

Girls and boys often share the same interests, study the same subjects in school, watch the same TV shows, read many of the same books. They have a lot in common besides sex, and throughout life many people have friends of the opposite sex.

What are good ways for preteens and younger teens to meet socially?

It's fun for preteens and younger teens to have parties with both girls and boys. As kids get older, small groups of boys and girls may meet at places like the movies or a skating rink.

·WHAT·IS·
·SEXUAL·INTERCOURSE?·

In school, Anne has heard kids making jokes about "doing it." She knows they are talking about sexual intercourse, and she pretends to know all about it. But at the same time, it's hard for her to imagine having intercourse, and she can't really understand why anyone would want to.

Anne is not alone in her feelings. Many kids don't really understand about intercourse, but they feel embarrassed about not knowing, so they pretend to know more than they do.

Why do people have sexual intercourse?

People have intercourse for several reasons. For one thing, sexual intercourse is the way a baby gets started, so when a couple wants a child, they make love in the hope that the woman will get pregnant. But people make love at other times, too, because it feels good and because it's a way to express their love for each other.

What happens when a man and a woman have sexual intercourse?

A man's body and a woman's body are made so that they fit together. Having intercourse means that the man pushes his erect penis into the woman's vagina. Then the man and woman move their hips so the penis will slide in and out. The movement of the penis feels good to both partners, and gradually the pleasure builds up until the man ejaculates and semen comes out of his penis.

This makes intercourse sound simple, but actually it is a very powerful experience between two people. Having intercourse is also called "making love" because a man and a woman usually feel so loving toward each other when they do it. They hug, kiss, and stroke each other's bodies. Both the man and the woman have strong sexual feelings of pleasure and a sense of closeness to each other.

Why is it hard for younger kids to understand why people make love?

When young children first hear about intercourse, they often think it is a weird thing to do. This is because they don't know about the *feelings* adults have when they make love. The actions of making love don't make much sense if you don't imagine the pleasure and love that go along with them.

Also, because a woman's sex organs are close to her waste openings, and because both urine and sperm come out of a man's penis, young kids may think that sex is connected in some way with going to the bathroom. Children may worry that a man could urinate inside a woman during intercourse. They feel better knowing that this is impossible; when a man ejaculates, only sperm can come out, not urine.

As people get older, they understand that sex and bathroom functions are different and separate from each other.

Can children have intercourse?

It is possible for some children to go through the motions of sexual intercourse. But children need to become adults before they are ready to have sexual relationships.

Do people still have sex when they get old?

Yes. Many people continue to enjoy making love for as long as they live.

What is a virgin?

Someone who has never had sexual intercourse is called a virgin.

· 52 ·

Do some people choose not to have sexual intercourse?

Yes. While most people do have intercourse, some decide not to. Some people are simply happier without sex. Others prefer to wait until they have fallen in love with the right person. Still others have religious reasons. For example, priests and nuns in the Roman Catholic Church take a vow as part of their religion not to have sexual relationships.

Do people have to be married to make love?

No. Some people believe that men and women who are not married should not have sexual intercourse, but many others do not agree with this. Men and women who are not married often make love, but most people believe that you should not do this until you are old enough to know how to prevent pregnancy, which can result from sexual intercourse, and how to protect yourself from certain diseases that can be spread through intercourse. Most people believe that you should make love only with someone you care about deeply and know well.

Do people ever make love with people they don't know well?

On TV and in the movies, you often see stories about two people who meet, are attracted to each other, and then make love right away. People don't act this way as often in real life as they do in the movies. In fact, this kind of behavior can be risky because of the possibility of pregnancy or disease.

Having sex right away also does not give people time to find out if they can really trust and care about each other. There are many ways other than having sex for people to enjoy one another's company. (To read more about avoiding pregnancy, see page 62. For more about diseases that can be spread through sex, see page 81.)

·HAVING·A·BABY·

Rebecca's married sister is pregnant, and soon there will be a new baby in the family. At first, Rebecca didn't think much about it, but as time went on, she began to get more excited. She likes to put her hand on her sister's abdomen and feel the baby kick. Now she feels it's somehow "her" baby, and she can't wait for it to be born.

What makes a woman pregnant?

When a woman has sexual intercourse, a sperm cell from the man's body may join an egg cell, or ovum, in the woman's body. When this happens, a new cell is formed that begins to grow into a baby, and the woman is pregnant.

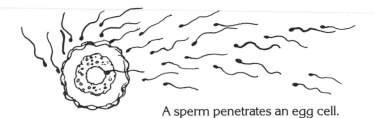

A sperm penetrates an egg cell.

Does a woman get pregnant every time she has sexual intercourse?

No. If an egg cell is not ready in the woman's body when she has intercourse, she will not become pregnant.

However, because it is hard to know exactly when the egg cell will be ready, there is a chance that a woman may get pregnant whenever she has intercourse. For this reason, most couples use birth control. This way, they can enjoy making love even when they do not want to start a baby. (To read more about birth control, see pages 62–68.)

Where in a woman's body does an unborn baby grow?

Young children often think babies grow in the stomach, and even adults sometimes say that an unborn baby is in its mother's "tummy." The baby actually develops in the uterus, or womb, which is a special part of the body for babies only.

How does a baby get food and oxygen in the uterus?

While the baby is in the uterus, the mother's body nourishes the baby. A flat mass of blood vessels called the placenta is attached to the side of the uterus. The placenta is the connecting site between the baby's blood supply and the mother's. Through the umbilical cord—a tube that stretches from the baby's navel to the placenta—the baby gets oxygen and nourishment from its mother's blood.

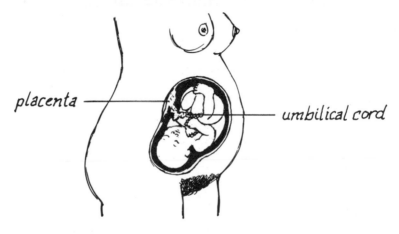

placenta — umbilical cord

Can a baby move in the uterus?

Yes. After about four months of pregnancy, the mother can feel little flutters in her abdomen. This is the baby moving. It can move its arms and legs, turn over, even suck its thumb in the womb. Others can feel the baby moving if they place a hand on the mother's abdomen. Toward the end of the pregnancy, the kicks are strong enough to startle the mother, but they don't hurt her. Most mothers are amused and pleased when they feel the baby moving inside.

Why are some babies boys and some babies girls?

The baby's sex is determined by the father's sperm. There are two kinds of sperm: Some sperm have the blueprint for a girl baby, other sperm have the blueprint for a boy. If a boy-making sperm unites with the egg cell, the baby will be a boy. If it is a girl-making sperm, a girl will be born.

How does a pregnant woman take care of her unborn baby?

A pregnant woman should see a doctor early in her pregnancy. She should eat wholesome food, drink milk, and avoid drinking alcohol and taking drugs. Even simple medicines like aspirin can cross the placenta and affect the baby, so a pregnant woman should not take any medicine without first asking her doctor about it.

How is a baby born?

When a baby is ready to be born, the mother's uterus—which is made of muscle—begins to squeeze. These squeezes are called contractions,or labor pains. Gradually, the uterus pushes the baby out and into the vagina, which stretches to let the baby through.

What happens if a baby can't come out?

If, for some reason, the birth is difficult, a doctor may perform an operation called a cesarean. The mother is given an an-

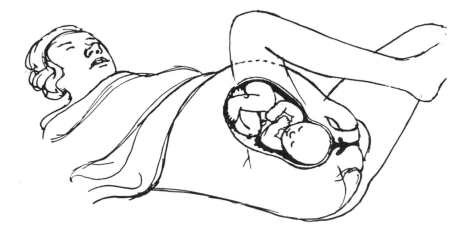

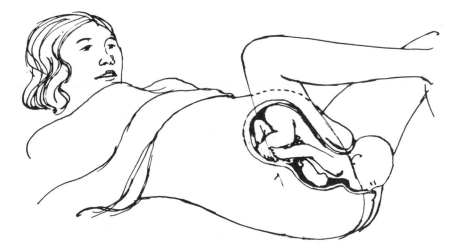

When a baby is born, the uterus contracts and pushes the baby out through the vagina.

esthetic, and the doctor cuts open the abdomen and uterus. The baby is then lifted out of the opening, and the doctor stitches up the incision so it can heal properly.

Does it hurt to have a baby?

Labor contractions—the squeezing of the uterus—can be painful. But most couples learn natural childbirth methods to help control the pain. After the baby is born, mothers are so happy that the pain does not seem important. Most mothers are smiling and happy as soon as their babies are born.

What happens to the baby's umbilical cord?

The doctor or midwife puts a clamp on the cord about two inches from the baby's belly. Then he or she cuts the cord. Because there are no nerves in the cord, it does not hurt the baby when it is cut. In a week or two, the stump dries up and falls off. Under the stump is the baby's navel.

Why can't some couples have children?

Some people are infertile, or sterile. This means that they cannot have babies. In women, a common cause for infertility is a block in the tubes leading from the ovaries to the uterus. In men, a common cause is low sperm count—too few sperm in the semen.

What are some ways for infertile couples to have children?

Many infertile couples adopt babies or older children. Others may go to fertility doctors to try to correct the problem. A woman can have an operation to open her tubes. If the man has a low sperm count, his sperm can be collected and inserted into the woman's vagina through a tube instead of through intercourse. Because the sperm is concentrated, there is more chance the woman will become pregnant. This procedure is called artificial insemination.

If the man has no sperm, or if his sperm are unable to penetrate an egg cell, the woman may be artificially impregnated with another man's sperm. If the woman cannot become pregnant, the couple may hire a surrogate mother—a woman who agrees to be artificially impregnated with the man's sperm and have a baby for the couple. Surrogate motherhood is still new, and there is a lot of controversy about it.

What is it like to be a parent?

Having children is a unique and wonderful experience. Parents love their children and enjoy them. But parenthood is also a lot of work. Parents must care for their children and give them the things they need. This is a big responsibility, and that is why people should think carefully before they decide to have children.

·HOW·DO·PEOPLE· ·PREVENT·PREGNANCY?·

Sally and Jim are a newly married couple on their honeymoon. They are enjoying being together and making love, but they feel they are too young to have a baby yet. They want to wait a few years before they start a family, so they are using birth control to prevent pregnancy.

What is birth control?

Birth control is any method a couple uses to prevent the egg and sperm from coming together during intercourse. Another word for birth control is contraception.

Which methods of birth control work best?

The pill:

A woman can take a pill that keeps her ovaries from releasing egg cells. Then it is very unlikely that she will get pregnant. She takes a pill every day. If she stops taking the pills, she will be able to get pregnant again.

Condoms:

The man puts a rubber sheath—a condom—over his erect penis before intercourse.

The diaphragm:

The woman inserts a rubber cap—a diaphragm—in her vagina each time she has intercourse. It covers the entrance to the uterus and keeps sperm from entering. To work properly, a diaphragm must be used along with a sperm-killing jelly or cream.

The "sponge":

Before intercourse, the woman puts a small disk of polyurethane—a contraceptive sponge—into her vagina. The sponge, which is treated with a sperm-killing ingredient, blocks the entrance to the uterus.

See the next page for pictures of products that work best.

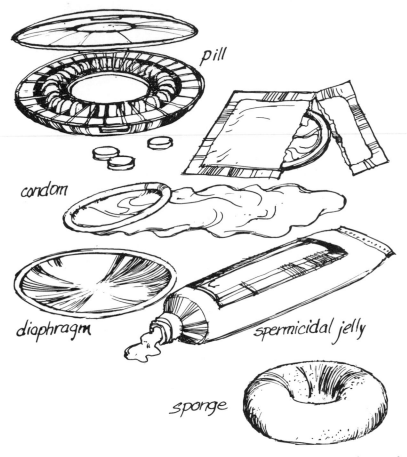

The most effective methods of birth control are the pill, condoms, the diaphragm, and the sponge.

How do people get birth-control devices?

Condoms, sponges, and jellies and foams are for sale in drugstores, and anyone can buy them. The pill or a diaphragm must be prescribed for a woman by a doctor.

People of all ages can get information and low-cost or free birth-control devices at clinics and Planned Parenthood centers.

Which methods of birth control do not work as well?

The rhythm method:

In this method, the couple tries to predict when ovulation—the release of the egg cell—will take place in the woman's body. Then they avoid having intercourse at that time. This method often fails because it is very hard to be sure when a woman is ovulating.

Foams and jellies:

A woman puts a sperm-killing foam or jelly in her vagina before intercourse. These do not work well unless a diaphragm is used along with them.

Withdrawal:

The man pulls his penis out of the woman's vagina before he ejaculates. This often fails because some semen may escape before ejaculation.

Does everyone use birth control?

No. Some religions teach that it is wrong to try to prevent pregnancy. They feel it is wrong to interfere with nature. The Roman Catholic Church, for example, forbids all birth-control methods except the rhythm method and abstinence—not having intercourse.

What is sterilization?

Sterilization is an operation to prevent pregnancy from oc-
curring. In a woman, a doctor cuts the tubes that lead from
the ovaries to the uterus so no egg cells can reach the uterus.
This operation is called a tubal ligation.

In a man, the doctor cuts the tubes that carry sperm from
the testicles to the penis. This operation is called a vasectomy.
Semen still comes out of the man's penis when he ejaculates,
but there are no sperm in the semen.

People who are sterilized still have sexual intercourse in the
same way. The only difference is that a sterilized woman will
not get pregnant, and a sterilized man will not make a woman
pregnant. For most people, sterilization is permanent; it is an
operation that cannot be reversed.

Once a woman is pregnant, is there any way for her to avoid having a baby?

Yes. A pregnant woman can have an abortion—a medical
procedure to end a pregnancy before the baby can be born.

Is abortion an alternative to birth control?

Abortion is a procedure that has risks, so people should not
think of it as just another method of birth contol. It is an
alternative when an unwanted pregnancy has occurred and
no other way of avoiding having a baby is possible.

Why does a woman have an abortion?

A woman usually has an abortion when she has become pregnant by accident and when having a baby would be a hardship. For example, pregnancy might be dangerous to her health, she and the father might not be able to afford to raise a child, or she might be too young to be a good mother.

Does everyone agree that abortion is okay?

No. Many people in this country believe abortion is wrong. Some people are against it for religious reasons. Others just feel it goes against nature to end a pregnancy. There are organizations that are trying to make abortion against the law again, the way it used to be.

Other groups believe that women have a right to make choices about their lives and their bodies. They do not think that anyone should be able to tell a woman that she must have a baby because she has become pregnant. They feel that this decision is a private one and should be up to the woman and her doctor.

There is a lot of discussion about abortion, and people on both sides feel very strongly about the issue. But right now the law allows abortion.

·WHAT·HAPPENS·
·IF·A·YOUNG·GIRL·
·GETS·PREGNANT?·

Ken and Sara liked to put their arms around each other and kiss. Then they started caressing each other under their clothes.

They both thought that they would be able to stop in time, so they did not have any method of birth control. But their feelings were so strong that they did not stop. They had intercourse, and Sara got pregnant. Now Sara knows that her whole life will change.

At what age can a girl get pregnant?

A girl can get pregnant around the time that she begins to menstruate. If the girl is eleven when she gets her first period, it is possible for her to get pregnant at eleven if she has intercourse. If she is fifteen, then she can get pregnant at that age.

Can a girl get pregnant from kissing or holding hands?

No.

Can a girl get pregnant the first time she has intercourse?

Yes. Many kids hear that you can't get pregnant the first time, but this is not true. Kids also hear that you can't get pregnant if you have intercourse standing up. This is not true either.

It is also possible for a girl to get pregnant even if the male pulls out his penis before he ejaculates. Some sperm may come out of the penis before the ejaculation.

Pregnancy may also happen if a male ejaculates while his penis is touching the *outside* opening of the girl's vagina. Some sperm may be able to enter the vagina.

What happens when a girl gets pregnant?

When a young girl has intercourse and gets pregnant, she has three choices. She can have the baby and keep it. She can have the baby and let a family adopt it. Or she can have an abortion. In any case, her whole life will change, and not usually for the better.

If she keeps the baby, it will be hard for her to finish school and do the things she had hoped to. If she has an abortion or gives the baby up for adoption, she may feel upset for a long time afterward. It is almost always better for young people to wait until they are older to have babies.

Why would a girl let herself get pregnant?

There are many reasons why a young girl might not protect herself against pregnancy. She might not know what causes pregnancy. She might believe a silly story about preventing pregnancy that she heard from other kids. Or she might just think, "It can't happen to me."

Sometimes a girl secretly wants to get pregnant because she wants a baby to love her. Babies *are* sweet, it is true, but the reality is that a baby needs to *get* more love than it can *give*. A girl who hopes that a baby will give her the kind of love she needs from her family and friends will probably be disappointed.

Sometimes a boy and girl decide to have intercourse, but they do not know how to practice birth control. They may think they are too young to get birth-control devices, or they may think their parents would not want them to use these devices. If kids *do* decide to have sex, almost all parents would say it is better for them to practice birth control than to take chances. Kids can buy condoms in a drugstore, or they can get confidential help by looking in the yellow pages of the telephone book under "Birth Control Information."

What is the one sure way to avoid pregnancy?

The surest way to prevent pregnancy is not to have intercourse.

·WHAT·IS·
·HOMOSEXUALITY?·

Beth's Uncle Jim has always been her favorite relative. He is kind, intelligent, and fun to be with. Beth knows that Uncle Jim has a love relationship with another man, whom Beth has always called "Uncle Bob." Her parents have told her that people like Jim and Bob are called homosexuals.

In school, some kids call homosexuals names and talk about them as if they are terrible people. Beth knows her uncle is a good person, and she gets mad because the kids don't understand.

What is homosexuality?

An adult who has sexual relationships with others of the same sex is called a homosexual. *Homo-* comes from the Greek word for "same," so homosexuality means having sexual relationships with people of the same sex as yourself.

Homosexual men and women are also called gay, and homosexual women are also called lesbians.

What is heterosexuality?

People who have sex only with members of the opposite sex are called heterosexuals, or straights.

Hetero- comes from the Greek word for "different," or "other," so heterosexuality means having sexual partnerships with members of the other sex.

What is bisexuality?

Bisexuals are adults who have sex with both men and women. *Bi-* comes from the Latin word for "two," so bisexuality means a lifestyle of having sex with members of both sexes.

Are there many people who are gay?

About five to ten percent of people—five to ten in every hundred—are homosexual.

Why are some people straight and others gay?

Psychologists do not really know what causes a person's sexual preferences. Some believe that whether a person is straight or gay depends on experiences in early childhood. Others think homosexuality might be an inherited, or built-in, preference. As of now, however, we simply do not know enough to say why some people are homosexual and others are heterosexual.

Is homosexuality a sickness?

No. People used to believe that homosexuality was a form of mental illness, but now psychiatrists say that it is not. Homosexuality is just one way people can express sexual love.

Can homosexuals choose not to be gay?

Homosexuals can choose not to *practice* homosexuality; that is, they can decide not to have sex with members of their own sex. But for most gay people, it is probably not possible to choose how they feel inside and which sex they are attracted to.

Can you tell if someone is homosexual just by looking?

No. Some people may say that you can tell gay people by the way they look, act, and dress. They believe that gay men look and act "feminine," while gay women are more like men. In fact, the majority of gay people do not look or act any differently from anyone else.

Have there always been homosexuals?

We know that there were homosexuals in ancient times and that in different times and places, people have had different ideas about homosexuality. In ancient Greece, for example, it was considered natural for boys and men to have homosexual relationships in addition to marriage with women.

Why do some people have negative feelings about homosexuality?

In our society, there are a lot of strong feelings about homosexuality. In spite of the fact that many homosexuals make positive contributions to our culture, many people fear a way of life that is different from theirs and have a negative image of homosexuals. Some people show hatred and even violence toward gay people.

Are straight people ever attracted to someone of the same sex?

Yes. Heterosexuals often have homosexual feelings, even if they do not choose to follow a homosexual lifestyle. Straight people, especially when they are growing up, have feelings for people of both sexes. It is not unusual for a preteen kid to have a crush on someone of the same sex.

Because there are so many negative ideas in our society about being gay, young people may panic if they have any feelings or daydreams about people of their own sex. Yet most of them will not end up being gay. Naturally, a small percentage will—about five to ten percent, as we mentioned before. But most will not. They are simply going through a stage of growing up.

Can homosexuals be married to each other?

No state in our country allows a person legally to marry someone of the same sex, but often homosexuals hold their own weddings and live together in a long-term relationship like marriage.

Can homosexuals be parents?

Yes. Sometimes a man or a woman who is already married and has children may decide to divorce and follow a homosexual lifestyle.

Sometimes, homosexuals who have never been married want to have children very much. They can adopt a child, or homosexual women may choose artificial insemination as a way of becoming pregnant and having a baby.

Researchers say that homosexuals can be just as good parents as heterosexuals.

·TAKING·CARE·
·OF·YOURSELF·

PROTECTING YOURSELF FROM SEX ABUSE

When Melinda was younger, a baby-sitter promised to let her watch extra TV if Melinda agreed to play sex games.

Melinda's parents had told her always to say "No" if an older person asked her to do something that did not seem

right, so she refused to do it. Later she told her parents about it.

When an adult or older kid gets involved in a sexual way with a child, it is called sex abuse. It is wrong for older people to get sexually involved with children.

What is sex abuse?

If an adult or older kid touches a kid's sex organs or makes the kid touch his or her sex organs, that is sex abuse. If someone hugs and kisses a child in a grown-up way and doesn't allow the kid to stop it, that is sex abuse. If an older person makes a child watch sex activities, that is sex abuse.

What is rape?

If someone uses force to make another person have sexual intercourse when that person does not want to, that is a very serious form of sex abuse called rape.

Who are sex abusers?

A sex abuser may be an adult, a teenager, or an older kid. It may be a man or a woman, a stranger, a family friend, or a relative—even a parent or stepparent. You can't tell from looking who is likely to abuse a child.

What is incest?

The word *incest* means sex abuse among members of the same family—brothers and sisters, or parents and their children.

What is the difference between "okay touching" and sex abuse?

A friendly kiss or hug from a parent, relative, or family friend is not sex abuse. It is good for people to show their love by touching each other.

Your feelings will tell you the difference between everyday hugging and kissing and sex abuse. Everyday touching feels happy, comforting, and good. Sex abuse feels "funny" and "not right."

How can kids protect themselves from sex abuse?

Kids have a right to say "No" loud and clear if someone tries to bully them into sex. Abusers can take advantage of a child who is afraid to say no and who won't tell. The best defense is to refuse to keep secrets. Say "No" and tell a trusted adult—a parent, teacher, doctor, or member of the clergy. Every kid has a right to grow up in charge of his or her own body.

If kids have been abused sexually, they should get help from an adult they can trust.

What should you do if you are sexually abused?

Even when children try to protect themselves, sex abuse can still happen. If something happens to you, do not let any feelings of embarrassment or fears of being punished stop you from telling someone what happened.

Sometimes children may feel it is their fault if an adult forces or tempts them to get involved sexually. But the kid is not to blame. The adult is responsible for what happened. It is very important for kids who have been or are being abused to find a grown-up they can talk to and to get help as soon as possible. A kid should not have to be alone with an experience like sex abuse.

DISEASES YOU CAN GET FROM SEX

Unfortunately, there are certain diseases that are spread through close contact during sexual intercourse. They are called STDs, which stands for "sexually transmitted diseases."

If a person has an STD, there may be itching or sores on the sex organs. Sometimes, however, there are no outward signs or symptoms. But in either case, a person who has an STD can spread it to his or her sex partners.

It is very important for people to go to a doctor or health center if they think they might have an STD. These diseases can be very serious.

What are some of the most common STDs?

Gonorrhea: caused by bacteria; may cause infertility; can be cured by antibiotics.

Syphilis: caused by bacteria; if untreated, can cause death; can be cured by antibiotics.

Herpes: caused by a virus; causes painful sores on the sex organs; cannot be cured, but sores can be controlled by a medication.

Chlamydia: caused by bacteria; may cause infertility; can be cured by antibiotics.

AIDS: caused by a new kind of virus; leads to death; cannot be cured.

Why is everyone talking about AIDS?

AIDS is a new disease and a very deadly one. The name AIDS stands for Acquired Immune Deficiency Syndrome. AIDS interferes with the body's system for fighting disease, so that people with AIDS eventually die because they cannot ward off illnesses.

How does a person get AIDS?

There are two main ways to get AIDS. The first way is to have sex with someone who carries the AIDS virus.

The other way is to come in contact with the blood of someone who has the virus. This usually happens when drug addicts share hypodermic needles. If a person who takes drugs shares a needle with someone who has AIDS, the AIDS virus can enter the bloodstream and the person can become infected.

Can you get AIDS from touching someone who has the disease?

No. Doctors say that the only ways to get AIDS are through sex and through the exchange of blood. No one has gotten AIDS just from talking with or touching a person who has the disease.

Can you tell if someone has AIDS?

No. People can carry the virus for years before they develop outward signs of the disease. Some people have the AIDS virus without knowing it themselves.

Do only gays get AIDS?

No. Anyone can get AIDS. Some people think only gays can get it, because in the United States, the disease spread first among homosexual men. However, no one knows exactly why this happened, since in some other parts of the world AIDS exists mostly among heterosexuals. Gays did not cause AIDS, but many gays are victims of the disease.

Can children get AIDS?

Some children do have AIDS. Some babies were born with AIDS because their mothers were infected with the virus. A few children got AIDS through blood transfusions that were given to them before people realized that transfusions could be a source of AIDS. Today the blood that is donated for use in transfusions is tested to make sure that it is safe.

How can people protect themselves from AIDS and other STDs?

Some people are so frightened of STDs that they say no one should have sex except married people. But most people realize that this is impossible—the drive for sex is very strong, and people will not stop making love even if it can be dangerous.

Therefore, doctors give the following advice to people who are having sexual intercourse:

—Use a condom when having sex.

—Wash your sex organs before and after sex.

—Don't have sex with someone you don't know well.

—Have a sexual relationship with one person only, one who is not having sex with others.

—If you think you might have an STD, see a doctor right away.

Are STDs a reason to be afraid of sex?

No, but they are a reason to be *responsible* about sex.

·THE·MOST· ·IMPORTANT·THING· ·TO·KNOW·ABOUT·SEX·

The most important thing to know about sex as you grow up is to respect yourself and others.

Respecting yourself means accepting your body, without thinking you are "bad" because you have sexual feelings. It means making your own choices about what you will and will not do and not letting others pressure you into something you know is wrong for you.

Respecting others means not trying to bully or tempt another person into having sex against his or her wishes. It means not teasing or making fun of others about sex. And it means not pretending you are in love with someone when you're not.

Preteens and teens who are able to follow these guidelines are less likely to be hurt and more likely to have happy love relationships as they grow into young adults.

·IF·YOU·
·HAVE·MORE·QUESTIONS·

This book tells a lot about sex and growing up, but it doesn't tell everything. If you have a question that isn't answered here, you can ask your parents or another adult you trust. And you can consult another book. There are many good books about sex for young people, and some of them are listed on page 6.

As you get older, you will have new questions because you'll change and you'll be faced with more decisions. Don't think that you've learned all there is to know about sex just because you've read this book, or because your parents told you about it, or because you had a sex-education course in school.

If you're like most people, you'll keep on learning about sex all your life. Sex is about people and love, and those are two subjects no one ever knows everything about.

INDEX
(with pronunciation guide)

INDEX

cesarean (seh-ZARE-ee-uhn)
operation, 58–59

chlamydia (clam-ID-ee-uh),
82

circumcision, 28, 29

clitoris (CLIT-er-uhs), 15, 20,
41

condoms, 63, 64, 72, 84

contraception, 63
see also birth control

crushes, 44–46
homosexuality and, 46, 76

curiosity, 10

dating, beginning of, 47

daydreams, 43

diaphragm (DIE-uh-fram), 63,
64

drug addicts, AIDS and, 82

drugstores, birth-control devices in, 64, 72

egg cells, 14, 20, 22, 56

ejaculation, 37–38
orgasm and, 42
in sexual intercourse, 52
sperm escape before, 65,
70

erections, 29, 32–33

families
sex abuse in, 79–80
talking about sex in, 2–5

foams, contraceptive, 65

foreskin, 28

friends of the opposite sex,
47–48

gay persons, 74
see also homosexuality

girls, 14–27

gonorrhea (gahn-ore-EE-uh),
82

growing up, 9, 10

growth spurt, 33

height
of boys, 33, 34
of girls, 20, 21

herpes (HER-peas), 82

heterosexuality, 74

homosexuality, 73–77
AIDS and, 83
bad feelings about, 74, 76
crushes and, 46, 76
definition of, 74
marriage and, 77
reason for, not known, 75

hormones, 9

hymen (HIE-muhn), 14

incest, 79

infertile couples, 60–61

inner labia, 15, 20

jellies, contraceptive, 65

jokes about sex, 45